96 FACTS ABOUT TIMOTHÉE CHALAMET

Quizzes, QUOTES, QUESTIONS, and MORE!

BY ARIE KAPLAN

ILLUSTRATED BY Risa Rodil

Grosset & Dunlap

GROSSET & DUNLAP
An imprint of Penguin Random House LLC, New York

First published in the United States of America by Grosset & Dunlap,
an imprint of Penguin Random House LLC, New York, 2023

Text copyright © 2023 by Arie Kaplan
Illustrations copyright © 2023 by Risa Rodil

Photo credits: used throughout: (filmstrip) Vadym Kalitnyk/iStock/
Getty Images, (skyline) halepak/DigitalVision Vectors/Getty Images;
13, 29, 45, 61, 73: (speech bubbles with question marks)
Oleksandr Melnyk/iStock/Getty Images

GROSSET & DUNLAP is a registered trademark of
Penguin Random House LLC.

Visit us online at penguinrandomhouse.com.

Manufactured in Canada

ISBN 9780593750926   10 9 8 7 6 5 4 3 2 1 FRI

Design by Kimberley Sampson

The publisher does not have any control over and does not assume any
responsibility for author or third-party websites or their content.

TABLE OF CONTENTS

Part I

GROWING UP IN THE CITY OF DREAMS

A Shooting Star

Over the past several years, Timothée Chalamet has become one of the great film stars of his generation. A serious actor who's often known for playing conflicted characters, he astounds audiences and critics alike with his ability to totally embody a role. To *become* the character he is portraying.

Perhaps you've seen Timothée as the haunted, brooding Paul Atreides in the dazzling, action-packed 2021 movie *Dune*. Or as Laurie, the romantic lead in the 2019 adaptation of the classic novel *Little Women*. But Timothée Chalamet didn't achieve success instantly. It was the result of much hard work and years of dedication to his craft.

FAST FACTS!

In 2020, Timothée posted a random photo of his pantry on Instagram. Fans were obsessed, because his pantry contained foods one wouldn't expect a movie star to have, like Kraft macaroni and cheese. The photo got over a million likes!

Timothée has a few nicknames, including Timmy, Teemo, and Tim.

A Family of Artists

Timothée Hal Chalamet was born on December 27, 1995, in New York City. Timothée's father, Marc Chalamet, is a journalist and was previously an editor who oversaw French publications for UNICEF. His mother, Nicole Flender, is a real estate broker and a former dancer who has performed in several Broadway musicals, such as *Fiddler on the Roof* and *Hello, Dolly!*

In fact, Nicole is not the only artist in her family. Her brother, Rodman Flender, is a writer, producer, and director. And her father, Harold Flender, was a screenwriter.

Timothée's older sister, Pauline Chalamet, is an actor and dancer as well. So when Timothée was growing up, he was surrounded by actors, writers, dancers, and filmmakers. He grew up in a show business family. And this most likely had an influence on his chosen profession.

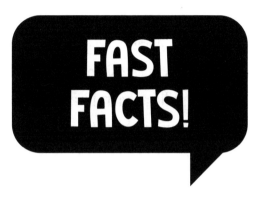

Pauline Chalamet made her television acting debut on the soap opera *One Life to Live* in 1999, a full decade before her brother, Timothée, made his TV debut on *Law & Order*.

Rodman Flender has directed episodes of many television shows, including *Gilmore Girls*, *The Office*, and HBO's *Tales from the Crypt*.

Summers in France

Timothée's father, Marc, was born in France, and when Timothée was growing up, Marc wanted him to be familiar with French culture, since that was part of his heritage. During the school year, Timothée lived in the United States. But during the summer, he lived with his father's relatives in the small town of Le Chambon-sur-Lignon, outside of Lyon, France. Because of that, Timothée is bilingual.

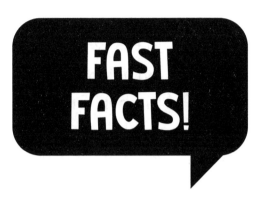

FAST FACTS!

Timothée has said that he really liked small-town life in France. However, it was a culture shock for him to come back to big-city life in Manhattan when the summer ended.

Timothée has dual citizenship in both the United States and France.

The Joker

Timothée grew up on the West Side of Manhattan, in the Clinton neighborhood, which is also known as Hell's Kitchen. Once a very dangerous neighborhood (hence its nickname), by the time Timothée was born, it was a considerably more friendly environment.

In 2008, when Timothée was twelve years old, he saw a movie that changed his life. That movie was *The Dark Knight*, and Timothée found himself riveted by Heath Ledger's performance as the Joker. Once the movie ended, Timothée knew that he wanted to do what Heath Ledger did: He wanted to be an actor!

FAST FACTS!

On that very important day in 2008, Timothée saw *The Dark Knight* after attending one of his sister Pauline's ballet performances.

Timothée had done some acting as a small child—mostly in commercials—but this was the first time he considered acting as a potential career.

1 Timothée's name is pronounced "Timothy," not "Tee-mo-tay."

2 Timothée is six feet tall.

3 When Timothée grew up in that apartment in Hell's Kitchen, he lived with his mother, father, and sister. Five floors below them—in that same building—lived Timothée's maternal grandmother.

4 Long before Timothée was born, his maternal grandmother was a Broadway dancer.

5 When Nicole Flender was a child, she danced at Lincoln Center with the New York City Ballet.

6 Timothée's aunt Amy Lippman is the cocreator of the television series *Party of Five*.

7 Timothée's zodiac sign is Capricorn.

8 Timothée's ancestry includes French (on his father's side) as well as Russian and Austrian (on his mother's side).

9 Timothée was obsessed with Power Rangers toys until he was around nine or ten years old.

10 Aside from Heath Ledger, another actor Timothée admires is Joaquin Phoenix.

Quickly or Slowly?

"Just like with acting, you have to grow up quickly in New York."

—Timothée on his upbringing

If you had a choice, would you grow up more quickly or more slowly? What would it be like to get older at an accelerated rate, or to grow up at a glacially slow pace? Write about it on the lines below.

_____

_____

_____

_____

_____

_____

_____

_____

_____

_____

_____

_____

_____

_____

_____

_____

_____

_____

_____

_____

_____

There's No Business Like It . . .

Timothée grew up in a show business family, surrounded by actors, artists, dancers, and writers. If you grew up in that sort of family, would you enjoy it? Or would it annoy you? Write about it on the lines below.

_____

_____

_____

_____

_____

_____

_____

_____

_____

_____

_____

_____

_____

_____

_____

_____

_____

_____

Quick Quiz: The Early Years

1) **Timothée grew up in an apartment building in Hell's Kitchen. What was that building called?**

   a. Avengers Tower
   b. Stark Industries
   c. Manhattan Plaza
   d. SHIELD Headquarters

2) **Timothée's sister, Pauline Chalamet, made her film debut with what movie?**

   a. *The King of Staten Island*
   b. *Toy Story*
   c. *Toy Story 2*
   d. *Toy Story 3*

3) **According to his mother, what stage play was Timothée's favorite when he was a child?**

   a. *Transformers: The Movie*
   b. *Slava's Snowshow*
   c. *My Little Pony: Friendship Is Magic*
   d. *G.I. Joe: The Rise of Cobra*

4) What is Timothée's maternal grandmother's name?

a. Marie Curie
b. Queen Cleopatra of Egypt
c. Joan of Arc
d. Enid Flender

5) When Timothée was a child, before he embraced a career as an actor, what did he dream of becoming?

a. A ghostbuster
b. A Jedi Knight
c. A professional soccer player
d. A Starfleet officer

Check your answers on page 78!

Part II

BIT PARTS AND BREAKING IN
The Big Audition

Now that Timothée realized he wanted to be an actor, he decided to go to a high school that specialized in the performing arts. He wanted to go to Fiorello H. LaGuardia High School of Music & Art and Performing Arts, which is located near Lincoln Center in Manhattan.

Many great actors, singers, and dancers have gone to LaGuardia High School, including rapper Nicki Minaj, *Friends* star Jennifer Aniston, rapper/actor Awkwafina, and *Buffy the Vampire Slayer* star Sarah Michelle Gellar. But in order to get into that school, you have to audition. Timothée auditioned for the school's drama teacher, Mr. Shifman. After the audition, Mr. Shifman gave Timothée the highest score he'd ever given to a student who was auditioning!

FAST FACTS!

During the audition, Timothée had to perform two monologues and a scene from a play, television show, or movie.

One of Timothée's fellow students at LaGuardia was the model and singer Lourdes Leon, daughter of the iconic pop star Madonna.

TV Time

When Timothée was very young—he's implied that it was when he was around four or five—he briefly appeared in a few television commercials.

But Timothée's debut as an actor on a television show happened in 2009, when he played the character of Eric Foley, the son of a pair of neurologists, on an episode of the police procedural series *Law & Order* titled "Pledge." He was thirteen years old.

Three years later, in 2012, while attending LaGuardia, Timothée snagged recurring roles on two television series. He portrayed an awkward, gawky character named Luke in four episodes of the medical comedy-drama *Royal Pains*. And he also played Finn Walden, the obnoxious son of the (fictional) vice president of the United States, in eight episodes of the spy thriller *Homeland*.

He was racking up impressive professional acting credits on respected TV shows. But more importantly, he was building a career.

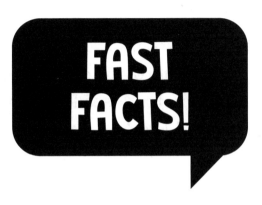

FAST FACTS!

Before appearing on *Royal Pains* or *Homeland*, Timothée appeared in a play called *The Talls* at Second Stage Theater Company in New York City.

Timothée was originally only supposed to be in one episode of *Homeland*. But soon, the producers put him in two episodes, then four episodes, and then eight.

The College Years

After graduating from LaGuardia in 2013, Timothée filmed a small role as a high-school football player in director Jason Reitman's movie *Men, Women & Children*. This was Timothée's feature film debut. He also played Tom, the adolescent son of the heroic astronaut Cooper (played by Matthew McConaughey) in the Christopher Nolan science-fiction movie *Interstellar*.

By the time both movies came out in 2014, Timothée had completed his first year of college at Columbia University. But he didn't enjoy going there. The classes seemed too rigidly structured. And so he transferred to New York University's Gallatin School of Individualized Study.

However, he soon dropped out of Gallatin to pursue acting full time. Would he regret that choice? Or would he make it in the acting world?

FAST FACTS!

The character Timothée played in *Men, Women & Children* was named Danny Vance.

Timothée only played the fifteen-year-old version of Tom in *Interstellar*. As an adult, Tom was played by Casey Affleck.

So Many Movies, So Many Genres

After a brief period of struggle—during which he wasn't booking many movie roles—Timothée's film career began to pick up steam, starting in 2015. Some of the roles he played during this period were minor supporting parts. But they were a good showcase for Timothée's talent.

For example, in the supernatural thriller *One & Two* (2015), Timothée played Zac, who discovers that he and his sister have teleportation powers. In the family comedy *Love the Coopers* (2015), he portrayed Charlie, an awkward teen experiencing his first romantic relationship. In the drama *Miss Stevens* (2016), Timothée was Billy, a rebellious kid who is mentored by a kindhearted teacher. Three very different movies. Three very different genres. Proof that Timothée could play a wide range of characters.

The only part Timothée hadn't yet played was a leading role. A role where *he* was the main character. But that would happen soon enough . . .

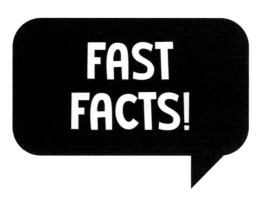

FAST FACTS!

Another film Timothée appeared in during this period was the drama *The Adderall Diaries* (2015).

One & Two premiered at the Berlin International Film Festival in February of 2015, before having a limited release in theaters.

Did You Know That . . .

1 Timothée's sister, Pauline Chalamet, also went to LaGuardia High School.

2 LaGuardia High School is sometimes nicknamed "The Fame School."

3 That's because the 1980 movie *Fame* is about aspiring actors, singers, and dancers who are attending the fictional New York City High School for the Performing Arts, which is based on LaGuardia High School.

4 While he was shooting *Interstellar*, Timothée became friends with that movie's star, Matthew McConaughey.

5 Timothée sometimes asks Matthew for advice.

6 Timothée's character in *Miss Stevens* is an aspiring actor.

7 In *Miss Stevens*, Timothée performed a monologue from the classic play *Death of a Salesman*.

8 *Love the Coopers* involves four generations of the Cooper family, who are getting together to celebrate Christmas.

9 In a surprise twist, at the end of *Love the Coopers*, it's revealed that the film's narrator is Rags, the family dog.

10 In *Love the Coopers*, Timothée and castmate Molly Gordon both have a funny running gag: Their characters (Charlie and Lauren) are both terrible kissers.

Believe in Yourself

"I have my teachers to thank for believing in me. They had faith in me. And eventually I started believing in myself."

—Timothée about his time at LaGuardia High School

Who in your life has helped you believe in yourself? A friend? A family member? A teacher?

_____
_____
_____
_____
_____
_____
_____
_____
_____
_____
_____
_____
_____
_____
_____
_____
_____
_____
_____
_____
_____

Superpowers

In *One & Two*, Timothée played someone who has teleportation powers. If you had a superpower, what would it be? Would you fly? Change shape? Run superfast? Write about it on the lines below.

_____
_____
_____
_____
_____
_____
_____
_____
_____
_____
_____
_____
_____
_____
_____
_____
_____
_____
_____

Quick Quiz: Paying His Dues

1) When Timothée was in high school, he created a music video as a project for his statistics class. In that video, he played a rapper named . . .

   a. Dracula
   b. Lil' Timmy Tim
   c. Frankenstein
   d. Mr. Hyde

2) Which superhero movie did Timothée audition for?

   a. *Spider-Man: Homecoming*
   b. *Romeo and Juliet*
   c. *Julius Caesar*
   d. *Macbeth*

3) During Timothée's first semester of college, Matthew McConaughey called Timothée and left a message on his voicemail to ask him . . .

   a. How to pilot a spaceship
   b. How to speak Martian
   c. How everything was going
   d. How to lasso a space creature

4) What famous sitcom is Timothée a fan of?

   a. *Waiter, Where's My Soup?*
   b. *Mmm, That's Good Soup!*
   c. *Oops, There Goes the Soup!!*
   d. *The Office*

5) When writing about Timothée's performance in *Miss Stevens*, a *New York Times* critic compared Timothée to the legendary actor . . .

   a. Mickey Mouse
   b. James Dean
   c. Donald Duck
   d. Goofy

Check your answers on page 78!

Part III

LEADING ROLES, LOVELORN CHARACTERS, AND LITERARY CLASSICS

Taking It to the Next Level

Timothée Chalamet was in four movies that came out in 2017. But only one of those movies truly took his career to the next level. Only one of those movies made him a star.

That movie was the romantic coming-of-age drama *Call Me by Your Name*, a film in which Timothée played the main character, a lovesick Italian French teenager named Elio Perlman, who lives with his parents in Northern Italy. In order to prepare for the role, Timothée learned to speak Italian, and he also learned to play the piano and guitar. Audiences were transfixed by Timothée's vulnerable, heartbreaking performance in the film.

Critics took notice as well, and so did Timothée's fellow film industry professionals. Timothée was nominated for a Best Actor Oscar at the 2018 Academy Awards for his role in the film.

FAST FACTS!

In 2018, Timothée—who was then twenty-two—was the third-youngest actor ever to get an Oscar nomination for Best Actor.

Timothée took his sister, Pauline, as his date to the 2018 Golden Globes.

Tackling Shakespeare

By the time he made *Call Me by Your Name*, Timothée had appeared in many different types of movies. But he'd never appeared in a Shakespearean period drama.

Then came the 2019 Netflix movie *The King*, which is an adaptation of three William Shakespeare plays, all artfully combined into one compelling narrative. In *The King*, Timothée played King Henry V, the charismatic English monarch who rallies an entire country to his side. Acting in an epic war movie was a new experience for Timothée, but you wouldn't know it, because he's so committed to the role, you'd think he'd been making Shakespeare adaptations his whole life.

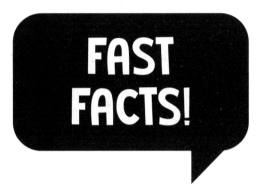

FAST FACTS!

Specifically, *The King* is a combination of the following three Shakespeare plays: *Henry IV, Part I*; *Henry IV, Part II*; and *Henry V*.

In the film, Timothée wears a short, cropped bowl haircut with shaved sides. Apparently, that's completely accurate, as it's the hairstyle the *real* King Henry V had!

Laurie the Love Interest

But *The King* wasn't the only 2019 film Timothée appeared in that was adapted from a literary classic. There was also *Little Women*. This was an adaptation of the famous Louisa May Alcott book about the brilliant and resourceful March sisters: Meg, Jo, Beth, and Amy.

Timotheé played a supporting role in this film, but it was an important one. He portrayed Theodore "Laurie" Lawrence, the childhood friend and neighbor of the March sisters. And at various points in the story, Laurie is the love interest for both Jo and Amy. In fact, he proposes to both women. Jo turns him down. Amy does not.

Timotheé made the character of Laurie both relatable and grounded, and in watching the film, one can see why he's such a big part of the March sisters' lives.

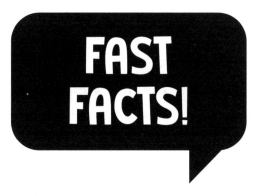

FAST FACTS!

Little Women was written and directed by Greta Gerwig, who had previously worked with Timotheé in the 2017 film *Lady Bird*, which she'd also directed.

According to the film's Oscar-winning costume designer Jacqueline Durran, when she was designing Timotheé's outfits, she kept in mind what she thought his young fans would want to see him wearing.

His First Blockbuster

By this point in Timotheé's career, all of his roles had taken place on Earth, in either the present or the past. Then he was cast in director Denis Villeneuve's 2021 sci-fi epic *Dune*, a movie that takes place on another planet, in the far future.

The film, based on the novel by Frank Herbert, is about Paul Atreides, the son of a duke who's given orders to preside over a desert planet called Arrakis, also known as "Dune." But an attack on House Atreides forces Paul to flee into the wilderness of Arrakis for survival.

Dune was Timotheé's first experience as the lead actor in a big-budget Hollywood blockbuster. As he told reporters, he felt a bit blindsided by how enormous of an undertaking it was to make the film. However, he eventually began to feel more sure of himself as he continued working on it.

FAST FACTS!

The 2021 *Dune* movie is actually part one of an enormous two-part film. As of this writing, *Dune: Part Two* is scheduled to be released in late 2023.

The director of *Dune*, Denis Villeneuve, has said that Timotheé was his first and only choice to play Paul Atreides.

Did You Know That . . .

1 In the original novel *Call Me by Your Name*, the character of Elio Perlman is not Italian French; he's simply Italian.

2 But when Timothée was cast in the movie version of *Call Me by Your Name*, the filmmakers decided to give his character partial French ancestry, just as Timothée himself has partial French ancestry.

3 Before *Call Me by Your Name* began shooting, Timothée arrived in Italy a month and a half early in order to give himself extra preparation time.

4 Aside from *Call Me by Your Name*, Timothée was in three other films that were released in 2017. They were *Hot Summer Nights*, *Lady Bird*, and *Hostiles*.

5 In *Lady Bird*, Timothée played Kyle Scheible, the snobby, cynical love interest of the film's protagonist, the sharp-witted, nonconformist teenager Christine McPherson, who has given herself the nickname "Lady Bird."

6 Timothée was in the first two films Greta Gerwig helmed as (solo) director, *Lady Bird* (2017) and *Little Women* (2019).

7 Timothée learned how to drive on the set of the 2018 film *Beautiful Boy*.

8 Timothée played the naïve, inexperienced soldier Private Philippe DeJardin in *Hostiles*.

9 *Hostiles* is a western about a group of US soldiers in the late 1800s who are escorting a Cheyenne chief across the West.

10 In 2019, Timothée brought a bag of bagels to the New York premiere of *The King*, and he gave them out to people in the audience.

A Fine Balance

"I do find that there's a fine balance between preparation and seeing what happens naturally."

—Timothée on acting

Can you think of a time when you felt it was important to do a lot of preparation in order to accomplish something? What happened? Did it go well?

And on the other hand, can you think of a time when you didn't do *any* preparation for the task at hand, and simply saw what would happen naturally? How did that turn out?

_____

_____

_____

_____

_____

_____

_____

_____

_____

_____

_____

_____

_____

_____

_____

_____

_____

_____

A Historic Journey

In *Little Women*, Timothée Chalamet and Saoirse Ronan played characters who are living in the 1860s. If you were living in the 1860s, what would be the best and the worst things about being a child during that time period?

_____

_____

_____

_____

_____

_____

_____

_____

_____

_____

_____

_____

_____

_____

_____

Quick Quiz: Bigger than Ever

1) In the film *Beautiful Boy*, who played Timothée's dad?

    a. Lucky the Leprechaun
    b. The Trix rabbit
    c. Steve Carell
    d. Tony the Tiger

2) In *Hot Summer Nights*, the character Timothée played is named . . .

    a. Daniel
    b. James Bond
    c. Indiana Jones
    d. Lemony Snicket

3) In *Hostiles*, Timothée's character, Private Philippe DeJardin, is from . . .

    a. Narnia
    b. Middle Earth
    c. Asgard
    d. France

4) What color is Saoirse Ronan's hair in *Lady Bird*?

a. Paisley
b. Red
c. Polka dots
d. Plaid

5) In *Dune*, Timotheé's character, Paul Atreides, is the son of . . .

a. Avatar the Last Airbender
b. SpongeBob SquarePants
c. Duke Leto Atreides
d. Tommy Pickles

Check your answers on page 78!

Part IV

FAMILY, FRIENDS, AND FASHION

Support System

As a young person in the entertainment industry, Timothée lives a life of long work hours and constant rehearsal. So it's good that Timothée has people he can turn to when he's overwhelmed, or when he simply wants to unwind.

For one thing, there's his family. He sometimes comes to his mother, Nicole, when he needs advice. It was Nicole's idea for Timothée to give college a try after he'd graduated from LaGuardia High School.

But who are the other people in Timothée's support system? And what does he enjoy doing in his spare time? What is he passionate about?

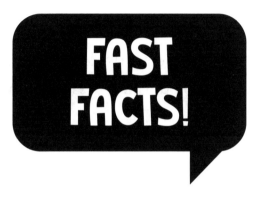

FAST FACTS!

In 2019, when Timothée was nominated for a Golden Globe Award for his performance in *Beautiful Boy*, he took his mother as his date to the awards ceremony.

In December of 2022, Timothée posted a silly selfie of himself and his dad, Marc, laughing together on Instagram.

Timothée and Cudi

After Timothée left NYU, there was a brief period in which he struggled. He went on numerous auditions but didn't get very many roles.

One day during that dry spell, he attended a Kid Cudi concert in Montreal. Kid Cudi was one of Timothée's musical heroes. After the show, Timothée hung out with Cudi backstage. Timothée told his hero about his stalled career. Cudi told Timothée about his own struggles early in his career; he had to work incredibly hard, but he eventually succeeded! Timothée left the show feeling truly inspired, and with a much more positive attitude about his career.

In the years since they first met backstage at that Montreal concert, Timothée and Cudi have become good friends. Both of them have spoken about their admiration for one another, and they've posted pictures of themselves hanging out on social media.

FAST FACTS!

Timothée and Cudi have also appeared together in a few film and television projects, such as the Netflix movie *Don't Look Up*, and the animated series *Entergalactic*.

Also, Timothée and Cudi have appeared together in Cudi's 2021 documentary titled *A Man Named Scott*.

A Mutual Appreciation Society

Timothée has acted alongside Saoirse Ronan in two films, *Lady Bird* (2017) and *Little Women* (2019). In both movies, Timothée played Saoirse's love interest. In real life, they're platonic friends.

In interviews, Timothée has said that he considers Saoirse one of his best friends. Why is that? Saoirse has said that she and Timothée look out for each other. She has also said that Timothée is very grateful and gracious toward the people he works with. For his part, Timothée has pointed out that he *is grateful* to work with Saoirse. And he's noted that Saoirse doesn't treat him in a judgmental manner. That sort of mutual trust, admiration, and support is the basis for a solid friendship.

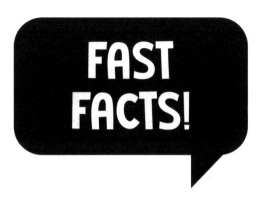

FAST FACTS!

Aside from *Lady Bird* and *Little Women*, Timothée and Saoirse *also* both appeared in the 2021 film *The French Dispatch*. However, in that film, they don't share any scenes with each other.

In *The French Dispatch*, Timothée played Zeffirelli, an overzealous student revolutionary in France.

A Passion for Fashion

Timothée is famous for his commitment to his craft and the emotional weight he brings to his characters. But he's also well known for his fashion sense. Clearly, fashion is his passion.

For instance, sometimes he arrives at awards shows wearing unusual outfits. In 2022, he showed up at the 94th Academy Awards wearing a sequined Louis Vuitton jacket with no shirt underneath. But he was so confident, so comfortable in his own skin, he was able to pull off the daring look.

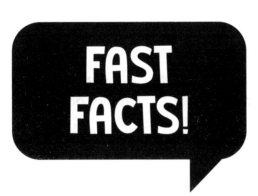

FAST FACTS!

It's because of Timothée's notoriously spot-on fashion sense that he was one of the cochairs of the 2021 Met Gala, where he arrived wearing a white satin tuxedo jacket, white sweatpants, and white Converse shoes.

In December of 2021, Timothée—working with Haider Ackermann—designed a hoodie. All of the proceeds from the hoodie went to the French organization Afghanistan Libre, which works hard to preserve the rights of women in Afghanistan.

1 Timothée's mother, Nicole Flender, has said that she always encouraged her son to pursue his dreams.

2 In the animated series *Entergalactic*, Timothée played Jimmy, the outspoken best friend to Jabari (played by Kid Cudi).

3 In October 2021, Timothée and Kid Cudi took a selfie together at the Met Gala.

4 Greta Gerwig has said that Timothée has such a wonderful sense of style that Jacqueline Durran, the costume designer for *Little Women*, just hung a bunch of costumes in his trailer and let him choose which ones he wanted to put together.

5 Jacqueline Durran has said that Timothée is one of the most stylish people she's ever met.

6

After shooting *Lady Bird*, Timothée and Saoirse Ronan hung out for much of the next year, solidifying their friendship bond.

7

During that time, the two also frequently saw each other on the awards show circuit, where Timothée was often nominated for *Call Me by Your Name*, and Saoirse was often nominated for *Lady Bird*.

8

During an *Entertainment Weekly* photo shoot in 2019 to promote *Little Women*, Timothée pranked Saoirse by sneaking up behind her and surprising her.

9

In 2019, Refinery29 compared the onscreen chemistry between Timothée and Saoirse to that of classic Hollywood couples like Fred Astaire and Ginger Rogers or Leonardo DiCaprio and Kate Winslet.

10

The section of *The French Dispatch* involving Timothée's character, Zeffirelli, was inspired by the 1968 *New Yorker* article "The Events in May: A Paris Notebook."

Attitude of Gratitude

"[I'm] grateful to get to work with her."

—Timothée about working with Saoirse Ronan on Little Women

Who are some of the people in your life you're grateful to know?

_____
_____
_____
_____
_____
_____
_____
_____
_____
_____
_____
_____
_____
_____
_____
_____
_____
_____
_____
_____
_____
_____

Flashy Dresser

Timothée really enjoys wearing flashy outfits and unusual-looking clothes. He likes experimenting with different looks. Do you like doing that? Or are you happier wearing the same types of clothes from day to day?

Think about a time when you tried to update your wardrobe or change your hairstyle. What happened?

_____

_____

_____

_____

_____

_____

_____

_____

_____

_____

_____

_____

_____

_____

_____

_____

Quick Quiz: Clothes and Camaraderie

1) Timothée has said that he wore his all-white ensemble at the 2021 Met Gala in order to provide a sense of ____ to the often-chaotic red carpet event.

   a. Smell
   b. Sight
   c. Sound
   d. Calm

2) When Timothée wore his shirtless Louis Vuitton suit to the 2022 Oscars, what did he wear on his fingers?

   a. Rings
   b. Magical gauntlets
   c. Alien oven mitts
   d. Mutated mittens

3) That Louis Vuitton suit jacket was covered in ____.

   a. Lobsters
   b. Melted cheese
   c. Sequins
   d. Chocolate

4) According to *Buzzfeed*, Timothée's Chinese fans sometimes call him "Tian Cha," which means what in Chinese?

a. "Shrek"
b. "Sweet tea"
c. "Donkey"
d. "Puss in Boots"

5) In 2019, Timothée said that working on *Little Women* with his friend Saoirse Ronan made acting ____.

a. Easier
b. Terrifying
c. Dangerous
d. Scary

Check your answers on page 78!

Part V

A BRIGHT FUTURE FOR A BRIGHT STAR

Comedic Commitment

Even though Timothée is famous for his work in powerful dramas, he's also a skilled comedic actor. As with his more tragic roles, he fully commits to his more humorous parts, making you feel that he *is* the character he's playing.

For example, in December 2020, Timothée hosted the legendary sketch comedy show *Saturday Night Live*. During the show, he played a variety of over-the-top characters. But perhaps the most memorable of these was the character he played in a pre-taped video called "Tiny Horse" (aka "The Farm"). In this video, Timothée played a farmboy who sings a farewell song to the miniscule horse he keeps as a pet. And what makes the short video so hilarious is Timothée's utter seriousness in the face of such a silly, absurd premise. He never once cracks a grin or breaks character. Critics were blown away by Timothée's performance, and *Paste* called "Tiny Horse" one of the best *SNL* sketches of the year.

FAST FACTS!

Timothée's stint as the host of *Saturday Night Live* isn't his only brush with comedy. *Love the Coopers* is a comedy, as is *The French Dispatch*, and he's very funny in both of those movies.

And in 2021, Timothée starred in a Cadillac commercial, where he played "Edgar Scissorhands," son of the legendary movie character Edward Scissorhands (from the 1990 film *Edward Scissorhands*). The commercial is full of slapstick comedy and silly sight gags, as Edgar (Timothée) deflates footballs and dices pineapples with his scissor-hands.

He's Got a Golden Ticket

Timothée is a movie star, and his star is constantly on the rise. What does the future hold for him?

Well, a couple of his upcoming projects have been announced. As of this writing, *Dune: Part Two* is scheduled to be released in late 2023. So is *Wonka*, a movie in which Timothée portrays legendary (fictional) candy manufacturer Willy Wonka. Both films mark new territory for Timothée. *Dune: Part Two* will be the first time he's been in a sequel. And *Wonka* will be his first children's film. So even in his forthcoming projects, Timothée continues to try new things and break new ground. His willingness to explore new styles and genres of storytelling is the very thing that makes him such a successful actor. One might say it's what gives him a Wonka-style golden ticket to greatness!

FAST FACTS!

The character of Willy Wonka was first created by author Roald Dahl for his 1964 children's book *Charlie and the Chocolate Factory*.

In *Wonka*, Timothée plays a *younger* version of Willy Wonka than the one we've seen in previous film versions of *Charlie and the Chocolate Factory*.

Did You Know That . . .

1 Timothée's "Edgar Scissorhands" Cadillac commercial first aired during the 2021 Super Bowl.

2 In that Cadillac commercial, Winona Ryder played Edgar's mother.

3 That's because Winona Ryder played Edward's love interest, Kim, in the 1990 film *Edward Scissorhands*.

4 Before Timothée Chalamet, the only other two people to play movie versions of Willy Wonka are Gene Wilder (in the 1971 film *Willy Wonka & the Chocolate Factory*) and Johnny Depp (in the 2005 film *Charlie and the Chocolate Factory*).

5 Like the 2021 *Dune* movie, 2023's *Dune: Part Two* will be directed by Denis Villeneuve.

6 Timothée's costars in *Dune: Part Two* will include Zendaya, Florence Pugh, and Austin Butler.

7 The character Timothée played in the 2021 movie *Don't Look Up* is named "Yule."

8 Yule is a shoplifter.

9 In 2023, Timothée made fun of his own earnest, openly emotional film persona in a commercial for Apple TV+ titled "Call Me with Timothée Chalamet."

10 In the commercial, Timothée is upset that Apple TV+ has called all of his friends and colleagues—like his *Dune* costar Jason Momoa—to star in films and TV shows for them. But they haven't called Timothée yet!

Wonka Wisdom

"Being okay with the weirder parts of you that don't quite fit in."

—Timothée on what Wonka is about

Were you ever in a situation where you felt like you didn't fit in? How did you react? Did any of your friends or family members help you to feel better?

_____

_____

_____

_____

_____

_____

_____

_____

_____

_____

_____

_____

_____

_____

_____

_____

_____

_____

_____

_____

_____

Far Future

If you lived in the far future, like the characters in *Dune*, how do you think your everyday life would be different than it is today? And what would remain the same?

_____

_____

_____

_____

_____

_____

_____

_____

_____

_____

_____

_____

_____

_____

_____

_____

ANSWER KEY

Pages 18–19:
1) c, 2) a, 3) b, 4) d, 5) c

Pages 34–35:
1) b, 2) a, 3) c, 4) d, 5) b

Pages 50–51:
1) c, 2) a, 3) d, 4) b, 5) c

Pages 66–67:
1) d, 2) a, 3) c, 4) b, 5) a

Arie Kaplan is a freelance writer. As a nonfiction author, Arie is perhaps most well-known for the acclaimed book *From Krakow to Krypton: Jews and Comic Books*, a 2008 finalist for the National Jewish Book Award. He has also written nonfiction books on everything from the history of piracy to the life of Vlad the Impaler.

In addition to his nonfiction work, Arie has penned numerous books and graphic novels for young readers, including *LEGO Star Wars: The Official Stormtrooper Training Manual*, *The New Kid from Planet Glorf*, *The Jurassic Park Little Golden Book*, and *Frankie and the Dragon*. Aside from his work as an author, Arie is a screenwriter for television, video games, and transmedia. Please check out his website: www.ariekaplan.com.